BASEBALL LEGENDS

Hank Aaron
Grover Cleveland Alexander
Ernie Banks
Johnny Bench
Yogi Berra
Roy Campanella
Roberto Clemente
Ty Cobb
Dizzy Dean
Joe DiMaggio
Bob Feller
Jimmie Foxx
Lou Gehrig
Bob Gibson
Rogers Hornsby
Walter Johnson
Sandy Koufax
Mickey Mantle
Christy Mathewson
Willie Mays
Stan Musial
Satchel Paige
Brooks Robinson
Frank Robinson
Jackie Robinson
Babe Ruth
Tom Seaver
Duke Snider
Warren Spahn
Willie Stargell
Honus Wagner
Ted Williams
Carl Yastrzemski
Cy Young

CHELSEA HOUSE PUBLISHERS

BASEBALL LEGENDS

BOB GIBSON

Bill Deane

Introduction by
Jim Murray

Senior Consultant
Earl Weaver

CHELSEA HOUSE PUBLISHERS
New York • Philadelphia

To Pam, a Hall of Fame wife.

The author is grateful to Mike Wendell, for his research assistance, and to Wes Parker, for his keen memory and insight.

CHELSEA HOUSE PUBLISHERS

Editorial Director: Richard Rennert
Executive Managing Editor: Karyn Gullen Browne
Executive Editor: Sean Dolan
Copy Chief: Robin James
Picture Editor: Adrian G. Allen
Art Director: Robert Mitchell
Manufacturing Director: Gerald Levine
Systems Manager: Lindsey Ottman
Production Coordinator: Marie Claire Cebrián-Ume

Baseball Legends
Senior Editor: Philip Koslow

Staff for BOB GIBSON
Editorial Assistant: Mary B. Sisson
Designer: M. Cambraia Magalhães
Picture Researcher: Alan Gottlieb
Cover Illustration: Daniel O'Leary

First Printing

1 3 5 7 9 8 6 4 2

Library of Congress Cataloging-in-Publication Data
Deane, Bill.
Bob Gibson / Bill Deane; introd. by Jim Murray
p. cm.—(Baseball legends)
Includes bibliographical references and index.
Summary: A biography of the baseball player who pitched the Cardinals to World Series victories in 1964 and 1967.
ISBN 0-7910-1177-1
ISBN 0-7910-1211-5 (pbk.)
1. Gibson, Bob, 1935 – —Juvenile literature. 2. Baseball players—United States —Biography—Juvenile literature. 3. Pitchers (Baseball)—United States—Biography—Juvenile literature. 4. St. Louis Cardinals (Baseball team)—History— Juvenile literature. [1.Gibson, Bob, 1935 –. 2. Baseball players. 3. Afro-Americans—Biography.] I. Title. II. Series.
GV865.G5D43 1993
796.357'092— dc20
[B]

91-28899
CIP
AC

CONTENTS

WHAT MAKES A STAR

Jim Murray

No one has ever been able to explain to me the mysterious alchemy that makes one man a .350 hitter and another player, more or less identical in physical makeup, hard put to hit .200. You look at an Al Kaline, who played with the Detroit Tigers from 1953 to 1974. He was pale, stringy, almost poetic-looking. He always seemed to be struggling against a bad case of mononucleosis. But with a bat in his hands, he was King Kong. During his career, he hit 399 home runs, rapped out 3,007 hits, and compiled a .297 batting average.

Form isn't the reason. The first time anybody saw Roberto Clemente step into the batter's box for the Pittsburgh Pirates, the best guess was that Clemente would be back in Double A ball in a week. He had one foot in the bucket and held his bat at an awkward angle—he looked as though he couldn't hit an outside pitch. A lot of other ballplayers may have had a better-looking stance. Yet they never led the National League in hitting in four different years, the way Clemente did.

Not every ballplayer is born with the ability to hit a curveball. Nor is exceptional hand-eye coordination the key to heavy hitting. Big-league locker rooms are filled with players who have all the attributes, save one: discipline. Every baseball man can tell you a story about a pitcher who throws a ball faster than anyone has ever seen but who has no control on or *off* the field.

The Hall of Fame is full of people who transformed themselves into great ballplayers by working at the sport, by studying the game, and making sacrifices. They're overachievers—and winners. If you want to find them, just watch the World Series. Or simply read about New York Yankee great Lou Gehrig; Ted Williams, "the Splendid Splinter" of the Boston Red Sox; or the Dodgers' strikeout king Sandy Koufax.

A pitcher *should* be able to win a lot of ballgames with a 98-miles-per-hour fastball. But what about the pitcher who wins 20 games a year with a fastball so slow that you can catch it with your teeth? Bob Feller of the Cleveland Indians got into the Hall of Fame with a blazing fastball that glowed in the dark. National League star Grover Cleveland Alexander got there with a pitch that took considerably longer to reach the plate; but when it did arrive, the pitch was exactly where Alexander wanted it to be— and the last place the batter expected it to be.

There are probably more players with exceptional ability who didn't make it to the major leagues than there are who did. A number of great hitters, bored with fielding practice, had to be dropped from their team because their home-run production didn't make up for their lapses in the field. And then there are players like Brooks Robinson of the Baltimore Orioles, who made himself into a human vacuum cleaner at third base because he knew that working hard to become an expert fielder would win him a job in the big leagues.

A star is not something that flashes through the sky. That's a comet. Or a meteor. A star is something you can steer ships by. It stays in place and gives off a steady glow; it is fixed, permanent. A star works at being a star.

And that's how you tell a star in baseball. He shows up night after night and takes pride in how brightly he shines. He's Willie Mays running so hard his hat keeps falling off; Ty Cobb sliding to stretch a single into a double; Lou Gehrig, after being fooled in his first two at-bats, belting the next pitch off the light tower because he's taken the time to study the pitcher. Stars never take themselves for granted. That's why they're stars.

SHOWDOWN

It might have been billed as the "showdown of the century." The opening game of the 1968 World Series was at hand, and each team boasted an ace pitcher who was about to be named his league's most valuable player (MVP) for the season. It was the first time in major league history that two MVPs would oppose each other in such a situation. This was not simply the St. Louis Cardinals against the Detroit Tigers—it was Bob Gibson versus Denny McLain.

Gibson was the hard-throwing right-hander for the National League's Cardinals; McLain filled the same role for the American League's Tigers. Each had dominated his league in 1968: Gibson won 22 games, including 15 in a row, struck out 268 batters, and compiled a phenomenal 1.12 earned run average (ERA)—the lowest in more than 50 years, and a mark still unmatched in the 1990s. McLain won 31 games—becoming the first 30-game winner since 1934—while striking out 280 and posting a 1.96 ERA.

The similarities ended there. Gibson, nearing his 33rd birthday, was a tested veteran; McLain was a 24-year-old prodigy. Gibson was a moody, competitive black man; McLain was a free-spirited white man. Gibson was a sleek all-around athlete who excelled in all facets of the game; McLain was a chunky, one-dimensional player, mediocre at bat and in the field. Gibson was a reclusive family man; McLain was known as a swinger, a free spender, and a nonstop talker—his teammates had nicknamed him Mighty Mouth because of his brash, outspoken nature. Gibson strummed the guitar at home; McLain played the electric organ at Las Vegas hotels.

Gibson downplayed the significance of the pitching matchup, saying, "To win I have to do my job against nine men, not one." McLain, on the other hand, boasted that he and the Tigers would not only beat Gibson and the Cardinals—they would "humiliate" them.

"Winning is important, not humiliating someone," responded Gibson. "I can't understand why a person would want to feel that way, but if that's the way he feels, he's going to get his chance."

With all the verbal sparring and advance hype out of the way, the two teams got down to business at Busch Memorial Stadium in St. Louis on Wednesday afternoon, October 2, 1968.

For three and a half innings the game lived up to all expectations. Gibson had allowed two hits and struck out eight Tigers, while McLain had permitted just one hit in the 0–0 pitchers' duel. Suddenly the Cardinals broke through with three runs in the bottom of the fourth, and after one more inning, McLain was out of the game.

But Gibson was far from through. He continued to overpower the Tigers with a blazing fastball and a wicked breaking pitch. He struck out

Gibson delivers the first pitch of the 1968 World Series to Tigers shortstop Dick McAuliffe. Turning in one of the most brilliant performances of his career, Gibson struck out 17 Tigers in the game—a World Series record—and led the Cardinals to a 4–0 victory.

at least one man in each inning, at one point fanning five sluggers in a row: Al Kaline, Norm Cash, Wille Horton, Jim Northrup, and Bill Freehan. Through eight innings, Gibson had a four-hit shutout going, and he had whiffed 14 batters—one short of the World Series record set by the Los Angeles Dodgers' Sandy Koufax in 1963. His teammates were aware that Gibson was closing in on the record, but following an age-old baseball superstition, they remained silent so as not to jinx him.

After surrendering a leadoff single in the ninth, Gibson struck out Kaline for the third time—the record-tying 15th K. Thinking only of getting the side out and winning the game and completely unaware that he was closing in on history, Gibson bore down and fanned Cash, also for the third time. Gibson waited impatiently for the ball to be returned as catcher Tim McCarver stood up and pointed to the scoreboard. The board flashed a message, informing the cheering crowd that Gibson had just set an all-time World Series record. Gibson turned around and looked at the message. Then he shrugged and went back to work. He blew away Horton for his 17th strikeout, establishing a record that has yet to be equaled. It was an epic performance, the crowning moment in a Hall of Fame career.

More important to Gibson, however, was that the Cardinals had won the first game of the World Series, 4–0. Bob Gibson had done his job.

A GHETTO YOUTH

Gibson performs some ballhandling tricks during his basketball days at Omaha's Technical High School. The teenager's hoop skills led to a college scholarship and a brief professional stint with the Harlem Globetrotters, but at the age of 22 he committed himself to a career in baseball.

Robert Gibson was born on November 9, 1935, in the black section of Omaha, Nebraska. His father, Pack Gibson, was a millworker who died three month's before Robert's birth. Gibson's widow, Victoria, who worked as a laundress, was left to raise seven children in a four-room shack. One of Bob Gibson's earliest memories was being bitten on the ear by a rat.

Young Bob was a sickly child, and few people expected him to survive into adulthood, much less become a professional athlete. He suffered from rickets, bronchial asthma, hay fever, and a rheumatic heart. At the age of three, he became deathly ill with pneumonia. As his older brother Leroy—better known as Josh—carried him to the hospital, Bob asked if he was going to die. "No, Robert, you're not going to die," Josh assured him. "And when you're well, I'm going to buy you a ball and glove." This promise, legend has it, inspired Bob to recover.

Josh was nicknamed after the legendary Negro Leagues slugger Josh Gibson, to whom the Omaha Gibsons were not related. Fifteen years older than Bob, Josh became a surrogate father to the youngster. "Josh was the most influential person in my life as far as becoming an athlete," Bob would later recall. "Probably a lot of the morals and values, and a lot of my thoughts, are a direct result of his teaching and training, just as a father would transmit those things to his son."

During Bob's adolescence, Josh would spend endless hours drilling his youngest brother in baseball and basketball fundamentals. It was during one of these sessions that Bob was struck above the left eyebrow by a ground ball, leaving a scar that he has carried ever after. By the age of 12, he was playing American Legion ball. He later reflected that if not for sports, he might well have followed the path to prison taken by many of his neighborhood companions.

As a freshman at Technical High School, Bob was still sickly looking, standing only 4 feet 10 inches and weighing a mere 90 pounds. He was turned down for football because of his size and was not allowed to join the baseball team, either. By the time he graduated, however, he had filled out and had become a standout in three sports. He led his basketball team to the state tournament, set a city indoor high-jump record in track, and made the all-city baseball team, playing third base and catching as well as pitching on occasion.

Bob received a few offers to play professional baseball after graduation. But none of them was very lucrative, and Josh convinced his brother to attend college instead. Bob hoped for an athletic scholarship, but those dreams were soon denied. His basketball coach, Neal Mosser, had written on his behalf to Indiana University, receiving the perfunctory reply: "Your request for an athletic scholarship for Robert Gibson has been denied because we have already filled our quota of Negroes." The quota, incidentally, was one. Bob had suffered one of his first and most bitter tastes of racial discrimination.

Finally, Omaha's Creighton University offered Bob a modest scholarship, and he eagerly snapped it up. Majoring in sociology, Bob focused his energy on sports rather than scholastics at first, struggling through his first year with Cs and Ds. He eventually improved both his priorities and his grades, finishing just six credits short of a four-year degree.

Bob worked nights at a gas station and spent his free time with Charline Marie Johnson, a niece of his brother's wife whom he had met during high school. Three years after their first meeting, on April 14, 1957, Gibson and Johnson were married.

At Creighton, Gibson became the first black student to play either basketball or baseball. Averaging better than 20 points a game, he broke every school basketball scoring record. As a switch-hitting center fielder on the baseball team, Gibson led the Nebraska College Conference in batting and led his team to a state championship.

Gibson (front row, right) appears an unlikely prospect in this photo of the Omaha Tech basketball squad. A sickly child, Gibson was still short and skinny as a freshman— but he soon developed into a powerful athlete and starred in three sports at Omaha Tech.

The day after his wedding, Gibson was scheduled to play for a team of college all-stars against the world-famous Harlem Globetrotters. The Trotters, as they are known, are made up of some of the most talented black hoopsters in the country. They tour the world, beating virtually every opponent in a highly entertaining fashion.

This game appeared to be a routine outing for the Globetrotters. They outplayed the all-stars for three quarters as Gibson sat restlessly on the bench. Finally, Gibson was inserted into the game, and he turned it into a personal show-case. Scoring 15 points in the fourth quarter, he led his team to a surprising 1-point victory. A representative of the deeply impressed Globetrotters offered Gibson a contract on the spot. He eventually agreed to play for the team in the fall and winter of 1957–58, at the rate of $4,000 for four months. But for the immediate future it was time to play baseball.

Gibson signed a contract to play for the St. Louis Cardinals' American Association (Triple A) franchise in his hometown. He received a $1,000 signing bonus and a $3,000 salary, figures that paled in comparison with the six-figure amounts being paid to other prospects at the time. Combining this with his basketball income, however, Gibson and his new bride would be fairly well off compared to the average young black couple during the 1950s.

The manager of the Omaha Cardinals was 45-year-old Johnny Keane, a quiet but strong-willed man who was to play a giant role in Gibson's development as a player and a human being. When Gibson reported, Keane asked the young player what position he played. Gibson did not know how to answer. Over the years, he had pitched, caught, and played the infield and outfield. Impressed by Gibson's arm, Keane decided to put him on the mound and leave him there.

Gibson's professional debut was less than impressive. He walked the first three batters he faced, and he had let in three quick runs by the time Keane strode out to remove him from the game. Instead of administering a tongue-lashing, though, Keane spoke gently. "That's pretty good for a first time," he said. "We'll get back to you later."

After 10 appearances with Omaha, Gibson had a won-lost record of 2-1, but he was suffering from control problems and posted a rather high ERA of 4.29 per nine innings. He was sent down to Columbus, Georgia, of the South Atlantic (Sally) League. The idea was to give him a little more seasoning, but Gibson later recalled the experience as "the worst of my life." It was his first stay in the Deep South, and he was not prepared for the harsh racial discrimination he found there. "One fan called me 'Alligator Bait,' " he later recalled. "I laughed. I had no idea what he meant. Later, I found out. Negro kids used to be tied to the end of a rope and dragged through the swamps, to attract alligators. The Negro kid would be pulled out of the water and onto the shore, and the alligator would come out of the water after him. Then they would catch the alligator."

Gibson compiled a 4-3 record and a respectable 3.77 ERA at Columbus. Combined with his Omaha performance, he ended the 1957 season with a record of 6-4 and a 4.02 ERA. He had struck out 49 batters in 85 innings, but he had walked 61. Although he had made progress, he still had a long way to go.

MAKING THE GRADE

When Gibson reported for spring training with the Cardinals in February 1958, the Cardinals general manager, Bing Devine, took him aside. Devine feared an off-season injury to one of his best pitching prospects, and he asked Gibson to give up basketball. Gibson agreed after negotiating some financial incentives. The highly competitive Gibson had been annoyed by the clowning often indulged in by the Globetrotters, but he had not wanted to jeopardize his family's financial security. During the off-season, Charline Gibson had given birth to the couple's first child, Renee; another daughter, Annette, would be born two years later.

After two weeks of spring training, Gibson was reassigned to Omaha. Despite a 3-4 record there, he showed improved control and a lower ERA (3.31), good enough for a promotion to the Rochester, New York, ballclub in the International League. He finished with a record of 5-5 at Rochester, with a fine 2.45 ERA. Overall in 1958, Gibson posted an 8-9 record. Most important, he had compiled an excellent 2.84 ERA while pitching at the top level of the minor leagues.

Gibson went to spring training with the Cardinals again in 1959, and this time he survived all the cuts. He made his major league debut against the Los Angeles Dodgers on April 15, hurling two innings in relief and giving up two runs. But after two more brief appearances in relief, he was sent back to Omaha for more work.

Hoot—a nickname Gibson had acquired after the old silent-movie cowboy star Hoot Gibson—went 9-9 for Omaha with a 3.07 ERA. Recalled by the Cardinals in midseason, Gibson made his first big league start against the Cincinnati Reds on July 30, 1959. He made it a memorable event, blanking the hard-hitting Reds for nine innings and earning a 1–0 victory. However, he followed this with some rocky outings, losing five straight decisions before turning in a complete-game victory over the Chicago Cubs. In his final appearance of the season, against the San Francisco Giants, he earned another victory in relief. Thus, Gibson finished his rookie year with a 3-5 record and a creditable 3.33 ERA.

In 1960, Gibson again started the season with St. Louis, and again he was sent to the minors for more polishing. At Rochester, he struck out 36 batters in 41 innings and posted an ERA of 2.85, earning a recall from the big club. This time he was in the majors to stay.

However, Gibson did not pitch well for the Cards in 1960, going 3-6 with a bloated 5.61 ERA. He suffered from his usual pattern of control problems and inconsistency. Of most concern was his strained relationship with Cardinals manager Solly Hemus. Expressing

Gibson enjoys a game of horseshoes in 1960 with (left to right) Cardinals pitchers Larry Jackson and Ernie Broglio, and coach Howie Pollet. After spending the bulk of three seasons in the minors, Gibson became a bona fide major leaguer in 1960, but he struggled with his control and feuded with the manager.

little confidence in Gibson, Hemus remarked, "You will never be a pitcher. All you do is throw, you never pitch."

Gibson saw more action in 1961, but his role was never clear. Sometimes he started, sometimes he relieved, and sometimes he went a week between appearances. Then, on July 6, Hemus was replaced by Johnny Keane, Gibson's first professional manager. It was a turning point for Gibson. "Hoot," Keane told him, "from now on you're in the regular rotation."

Gibson wound up pitching 211 innings in 1961. His record was a modest 13-12, and he led the National League with 119 walks, but his 3.24 ERA was the best for any pitcher in the league. Opposing hitters, including future Hall of Famers Ernie Banks and Willie Mays, were impressed. "For 'natural stuff,' Gibson is it," said Banks. "He's the toughest in the league," added Mays. "When he starts believing it, he'll be great."

After playing winter ball in the off-season, Gibson showed even further development in 1962. Adding an effective curveball to his repertoire, he dropped his ratio of walks per nine innings from 5.1 to 3.7. His ERA dropped as well, to an impressive 2.85. He struck out 208 batters and tied for the league lead with five shutouts. In July, he hurled three consecutive three-hit games and was picked for the All-Star Team. But in the last two months of the season, Gibson ran into hard luck. Although he continued to pitch well, he dropped seven of his last nine decisions and finished at 15-13. Then, on September 21, his season was ended by a broken right ankle, suffered when he caught his spikes in the turf during batting practice.

The year 1963 was to be the crossroads in Gibson's career. At age 27, despite evident talent, Gibson had lost more games in the pros than he had won, and now he was coming off a major injury. Favoring his sore ankle, he had a record of 1-3 on May 23.

But once he was finally convinced that his ankle was sound, Gibson was sensational for the rest of the year. He won 17 of his last 23 decisions to finish with an 18-9 mark. He struck out 204 and was the leader of the pitching staff on a team that finished second, six games behind the Dodgers—the strongest finish for a Cardinals team since 1949.

Gibson was still rolling as the 1964 campaign got under way, winning his first four decisions for the pennant-contending Cards. Then, hampered by a tender arm at midseason, Gibson was battered for six runs in each of five straight outings, dropping his record to 8-9 in early August. There were whispers that Gibson was hurting the team's pennant chances and that he should be dropped from the rotation, but his manager gave him a vote of confidence. "If we're going to get anywhere in this pennant race," said Keane, "we're going to have to do it with Gibson."

During the season's last two months, Gibson was virtually unhittable. Striking out 112 batters in 119 innings, he posted an 11-3 record with a 2.20 ERA, practically carrying his club to the National League pennant. In the last 11 days of the season, Gibson hurled 29 innings and won three games, including the pennant clincher on the final day. As many as six games behind on September 21, the Cardinals roared up from third place to take their first pennant in 18 years.

Gibson finished the 1964 season with a club-record 245 strikeouts, a 3.01 ERA, and a 19-12 record. He might have won 20 except for a failure to control his temper: on May 4, he held a 7–1 lead over the Philadelphia Phillies after four innings, one short of qualifying for the victory, only to be ejected from the game for throwing his bat.

The 1964 World Series opened in St. Louis on October 7, and the Cardinals drew first blood with a 9–5 victory over the mighty New York Yankees, winners of 29 American League pennants in 44 years. The weary Gibson was called upon to start Game 2 the following day. Trailing

Gibson fans Yankees slugger Roger Maris in Game 2 of the 1964 World Series. Although the Yankees bested Gibson in the contest, he came back to win Games 5 and 7 as the underdog Cardinals stormed to the world championship.

4–1, Gibson was lifted for a pinch-hitter in the eighth inning, and the Cards went on to lose by a score of 8–3.

As the Series moved to New York, the Yanks scored a 2–1 victory in Game 3, but the Cardinals evened things with a 4–3 win the next day. Then it was Gibson's turn again.

Gibson pitched brilliantly in Game 5, taking a 2–0 lead and 11 strikeouts into the bottom of the ninth. With one out and a runner on first, there followed what many observers called the pivotal play of the Series. The Yankees' Joe Pepitone hit a line drive that smashed off Gibson's right hip and caromed toward the third-base line, an apparent infield hit. But the agile Gibson recovered, pounced on the ball, and threw an off-balance strike to first, getting

Pepitone by an eyelash. When Tom Tresh hit Gibson's next pitch into the seats, the score was tied—but had Pepitone reached first safely, the Yankees would have had a 3–2 win. Instead, Cardinals catcher Tim McCarver hit a three-run homer in the next frame, and Gibson and the Redbirds went home with a 10-inning, 5–2 victory.

The Yankees rebounded to win Game 6, 8–3, and it all came down to one game, which took place on October 15 at St. Louis. Johnny Keane's pitching choice—despite his having had only two days' rest—was Bob Gibson.

Gibson pitched heroically, taking a 6–0 lead into the sixth inning. A three-run homer closed the gap to 6–3, but then Gibson bore down to retire 10 of the next 12 batters. He entered the ninth inning with a 7–3 lead.

By now, the exhausted Gibson was pitching on guts alone. "I felt like I'd been in a gang fight," he said later, "and I was the only guy in my gang." Two Yankees home runs made the score 7–5, bringing up the leading hitter in the Series, Bobby Richardson, with two out. All eyes focused on Keane in the dugout, but he did not come out to make a pitching change. Gibson retired Richardson on a pop-up, the Cardinals took the world championship, and Gibson—who set a World Series record with 31 strikeouts—was named MVP of the Fall Classic.

With the Series on the line, why had the skipper not replaced Gibson? In a classic tribute from a manager to a star player, Keane explained: "I had a commitment to his heart."

4

STARDOM

Recovering from a broken fibula midway in the 1967 season, Gibson sports a sign containing answers to reporters' constant questions about his injury. After being sidelined for several weeks, Gibson returned in September and spearheaded the Redbirds' march to another world championship.

The 1964–65 off-season was a bittersweet one for Gibson. He received a new Chevrolet Corvette from *Sport* magazine for being named MVP of the World Series, and he was given the key to the city in a warm hometown reception in Omaha. But he was shocked when the fatherly Keane resigned as Cardinals manager following the Series, as a result of differences with the team's front office. Gibson soon had his own troubles with the St. Louis management, calling their first 1965 contract offer "an insult."

In those days, a big league player did not have the options of free agency or arbitration; he either had to come to terms with his team's management or sit out the season. The average major league salary was less than $20,000, and multiyear contracts were almost unheard of. Gibson finally signed a pact for $39,500, vowing that he would someday reach the $100,000 level—a salary no pitcher had ever attained.

On the field in 1965, Gibson picked up right where he had left off. Winning his first eight decisions, he reached the coveted 20-win mark

Entertaining his team-mates after a Cardinals victory, Gibson mimics a batter hitting the dirt to avoid a knockdown pitch. The routine would not have drawn many laughs in other clubhouses, where Gibson was known as a merciless competitor who loved to fire the ball high and inside.

for the first time, even though his club dropped all the way to seventh place (in a 10-team league) under new manager Red Schoendienst. Gibson struck out a career-high 270 batters, had a 3.07 ERA, and pitched two scoreless innings in his second All-Star Game.

Showing his tremendous athletic ability, Gibson also continued to excel as a fielder, hitter, and baserunner. He won his first Gold Glove Award, presented annually in each league to the players judged by their peers to be the best fielders at each position. Former Los Angeles first baseman Wes Parker, himself a six-time Gold Glover, recalled one of Gibson's outstanding plays: "Gibson had that follow-through where he'd be almost falling over to his left [toward first base] after he threw. Well, we had a runner on third . . . and the batter hit a slow chopper down the third-base line. Gibson took what seemed like four giant strides, gloved the ball, dove, and tagged the runner coming home. I never will forget that play."

Gibson, who once drew a pair of eyes on the barrel of his bat so it "could see the ball better," had little trouble swinging it. While most pitchers bat between .100 and .150 with no power, Gibson hit .240 in 1965, with 5 home runs and 19 RBIs. For his career, he would bat .206 (including .237 as a pinch-hitter), with 24 homers—the seventh-best total among pitchers in the history of baseball.

Despite elbow trouble that sidelined him for two weeks, Gibson enjoyed another banner season in 1966. He won 21 games for the sixth-place Cards, increasing his victory total for the sixth consecutive season: from 3 wins in 1960 to 13, 15, 18, 19, 20, and 21 in succeeding years. In 1966, he posted a league-leading total of five shutouts and compiled an outstanding 2.44 ERA. Gibson benefited both from improved control—just 2.5 walks per nine innings—and a larger stadium. (In May, the Cardinals had moved from their cozy old ballpark to the spacious new Busch Memorial Stadium.) On June 7, Gibson tied a major league record with four strikeouts in one inning—one victim reached first base when the third strike got away from the catcher. He also won his second Gold Glove in 1966. Gibson had now established himself as an all-around major league star.

Gibson started the 1967 campaign in a blaze. On opening day, April 11, he struck out the first five San Francisco Giants to face him, including future Hall of Famers Willie Mays and Willie McCovey. He wound up spinning an 8–0 shutout with 13 strikeouts.

Pitching every fifth day to lessen the strain on his arm, Gibson continued to rank among the league's premier hurlers. By midseason he was halfway to his annual goal of 20 victories, and the Cardinals were in first place. On July 11, Gibson appeared in his third All-Star Game, tossing two innings of shutout ball. Then, on July 15, calamity struck.

Gibson took the mound against the Pittsburgh Pirates that day, carrying a no-hitter into the fourth inning. Roberto Clemente, one of the league's most dangerous hitters, led off the frame, promptly lining a shot back through the box. The ball rocketed into the lower part of Gibson's right leg, making a loud crack. Gibson dropped to the ground and writhed in pain. He was not yet aware of it, but the drive had cracked his fibula, one of the bones between the knee and the ankle.

"Just put a little tape on it, Doc," Gibson told

Gibson gets a taste of his own medicine in Game 4 of the 1967 World Series as he ducks an inside delivery from Boston Red Sox hurler Jerry Stephenson. Gibson made this edition of the Fall Classic his personal showcase, winning three games and allowing a total of only three runs.

Bob Bauman, the club's trainer, who sprinted out to the mound, "and I'll be ready to go again." Gibson got back on the rubber, walked Willie Stargell, and retired Bill Mazeroski on a fly ball. Then, with a 3-2 count on Donn Clendenon, Gibson "tried to put something extra" on the payoff pitch. The hard follow-through was too much for the cracked bone, and Gibson collapsed with a broken leg. After examining the fallen hurler, team physician I. C. Middleman broke the bad news: Gibson would be sidelined until September.

The following weeks were torture for Gibson. He limped around the clubhouse in his cast and crutches, feeling helpless over his inability to contribute to the team's pennant drive. After the cast was finally removed on August 7, he found himself constantly answering the same questions from reporters about his recovery. Exasperated, he began wearing a sign around his neck, reading:

1. Yes, it's off!
2. No, it doesn't hurt.
3. I'm not supposed to walk on it for a week.
4. I don't know how much longer.
5. Ask Doc Bauman.
6. Ask Doc Middleman.

The sign was really meant as a joke, but some writers failed to see the humor. Gibson had a reputation for being moody with the media, and this only added to it. Finally, on September 7, Gibson was ready to get back into action. Facing the New York Mets, he lasted five innings, long enough to earn his first victory in 66 days, by a score of 9–2.

Gibson lasted into the seventh inning of his next assignment, another win, and then went the distance in his next outing—the Cardinals'

Fleet-footed Cardinals outfielder Lou Brock scores a run during Game 6 of the 1967 World Series. With standout players such as Brock, Curt Flood, Orlando Cepeda, Tim McCarver, Dal Maxvill, Julian Javier, and Mike Shannon in their lineup, the Cardinals captured three pennants and two world championships between 1964 and 1968.

pennant clincher on September 18. In all, he made five appearances in September, going 3-1 with an amazing 0.96 ERA. Gibson was definitely back, and the Redbirds were once again National League champions.

The Cardinals opened the 1967 World Series against the Red Sox in Boston's Fenway Park on October 4. Gibson pitched a complete game, giving up six hits and striking out 10, to gain a 2–1 victory.

The teams split the next two games, and Gibson started Game 4 at St. Louis. He came through with a five-hit, 6–0 shutout, bringing the Cards within one game of a world championship. He hoped it would be his last outing.

It was not. The plucky Red Sox rallied to win the next two contests, sending the Series to the deciding seventh game. It would be Gibson, on three days' rest, against Boston ace Jim Lonborg, who had had only two. Lonborg had won 22 games during the regular season and had throttled the Cards in Games 2 and 5, permitting just four hits in 18 innings.

Game 7 was all Bob Gibson. He homered off Lonborg in the fifth and held the Sox to three hits while fanning 10, posting a 7–2 victory and bringing the Cards another world championship. With a record of 3-0 and a 1.00 ERA, Gibson was named World Series MVP for the second time in four years.

5

AN EPIC SEASON

The 1967–68 off-season was one of collecting awards and honors for Gibson: another Corvette from *Sport*; the October Hickok Award; his third Gold Glove; the J. Roy Stockton Award for "outstanding achievement in baseball"; the Spink "St. Louis Man of the Year" citation; and even an invitation to the White House, where he joined President Lyndon B. Johnson and other special guests for a state dinner on November 14.

In February, Gibson signed a contract calling for a hefty raise, from $55,000 to $90,000. In spring training, he was unbeatable, logging a 4-0 record and a 1.64 ERA. This set the stage for one of the most remarkable individual pitching seasons in baseball history: Bob Gibson would go through the entire 1968 campaign with an ERA of 1.12, the lowest ever for a man hurling at least 300 innings.

Nevertheless, Gibson was also a hard-luck pitcher in 1968. His first regular-season appearance (April 10 against Atlanta) would prove typical: He allowed just three hits and one unearned run in seven innings but did not get a decision; his team was held hitless for five innings and scoreless for seven, and Gibson was removed for

Gibson tosses his 13th shutout of the 1968 season on September 26, blanking the Houston Astros, 1–0. Gibson finished the season with 22 wins and a phenomenal 1.12 ERA, the lowest in more than 50 years.

a pinch-hitter. He got another no-decision against the Braves five days later, giving up three runs in seven frames before being pinch-hit for. The Cards rallied to win, but Gibson did not get the victory.

Gibson's first decision, on April 20, turned out to be a loss, as the Cubs' Ferguson Jenkins spun a three-hitter against the Cardinals. Gibson did not crack the win column until April 26, with a 2–1 victory over Pittsburgh. The victory appeared to get him untracked, and he followed up with exra-inning wins over Houston and New York in which he permitted only 10 hits and 1 earned run in 23 innings.

Then came four frustrating defeats in a row, one at the hands of the Dodgers' Don Drysdale, who bettered Gibson's one-hit, one-run performance by tossing the third of a record six straight shutouts. Despite a splendid 1.52 ERA through his first 10 appearances, Gibson sported a meager 3-5 record. The Cardinals had scored a total of just 12 runs behind him, but Gibson refused to complain. He pointed out that the team had supported him well in the past, and that "you have to win your share of those 2–1 and 1–0 games."

Finally, the Cards came up with some runs to help Gibson to a 6–3 win over the Mets on June 2. During the next two months, it would barely matter what his teammates did, because Robert Gibson was simply untouchable.

Starting off what may be the greatest pitching streak in the game's history, Gibson shut out Houston on three hits on June 6. He then blanked Atlanta on five hits (June 11), Cincinnati on four (June 15), Chicago on five (June 20), and Pittsburgh on four (June 26).

This gave him a string of 47 consecutive score-less innings, and he was challenging Drysdale's record of 58, set just a month earlier. It was no surprise that Gibson was named National League Player of the Month for June, receiving 43 of a possible 50 votes, after going 6-0 with an 0.50 ERA.

A two-out wild pitch in the first inning of his next start (July 1, against Drysdale and the Dodgers) broke the scoreless streak. It was a low fastball—"a catchable ball," according to the Dodgers' Wes Parker—that eluded catcher John Edwards, allowing a baserunner to score. Undaunted, Gibson whitewashed L.A. the rest of the way to win, 8–1, and start another scoreless string: 23 innings this time, giving him 71 straight frames without allowing an RBI. He shut out Juan Marichal and the Giants on July 6, then three-hit Houston, 7–1, on July 12, pitching perfect ball for five innings. The Astros' run scored on a looper by Dennis Menke that landed just inside the left-field foul line.

On July 17, the Giants paid Gibson the supreme tribute when they scratched their own ace, Marichal, who had been scheduled to oppose him. Why waste Marichal, the thinking went, when Gibson was virtually unbeatable? The move paid off for San Francisco: Gibson had a 6–0 lead after four innings when the game was rained out, short of an official contest, and Marichal came back to win the next day.

Four days later, the Mets imitated the strat-egy by replacing scheduled starter Jerry Koosman with a minor league recruit. Gibson defeated the Mets, 2–0 (not allowing a single outfield putout), and Koosman beat the Cards the next day.

Gibson notched another shutout, against the Phillies on July 26, then beat New York four days later, 7–1. The Mets' run ended a period of 99 innings (counting the 4-inning washout) in which Gibson had surrendered just two other runs, both flukish. Had Edwards stopped the low fastball and had Menke's bloop landed a few inches to the left, Gibson could conceivably have rolled up 10 straight shutouts and 95 consecutive scoreless innings.

For July, Gibson was once again 6-0 with an 0.50 ERA, lowering his season mark to a staggering 0.96. Polling 45 of 50 votes, he became

Mickey Lolich of the Detroit Tigers prepares to deliver a pitch during the 1968 World Series. Gibson won two games for the favored Cardinals, but Lolich emerged as the dominant pitcher of the Series, winning three games and stifling the Redbirds in the finale.

the first man ever to be named Player of the Month twice in succession.

In early September, after a 10-inning, 1–0 shutout against the Reds, Gibson lowered his season ERA to 0.99 and had 20 wins against 6 losses. When a teammate suggested that he might catch N.L. victory leader Marichal, he was relaxed enough to put the needle in. "Not if you guys keep getting only one run a game!" he shot back.

As it happened, Gibson dropped three of his next four decisions, including 3–2 losses to San Francisco and Los Angeles and a real heart-breaker to the Giants on September 17: Gaylord Perry no-hit the Cardinals, Ron Hunt hit one of his two 1968 home runs, and Gibson lost, 1–0. Sandwiched in between was a 5–4 triumph over the Dodgers on September 11.

In his last regular-season appearance for the N.L. champion Cardinals (September 27), Gibson spun a 1–0 shutout over the Astros. It was his 13th, and with a few breaks, he might have challenged Grover Cleveland Alexander's all-time record of 16 shutouts in a season, set back in 1916. In 2 of Gibson's 11 one-run games, the tally had been unearned, and in another it had scored in extra innings (not to mention the other potential shutouts lost under freakish circumstances).

Gibson's final numbers were astonishing. He completed 28 of 34 starts, never being knocked out of the box but only being removed on six occasions for a pinch-hitter. In 305 innings, he gave up just 198 hits and 62 walks while leading the league with 268 strikeouts. He posted a 1.41 ERA at home and an 0.79 ERA on the road. His season's record was 22-9, but had the Cardinals

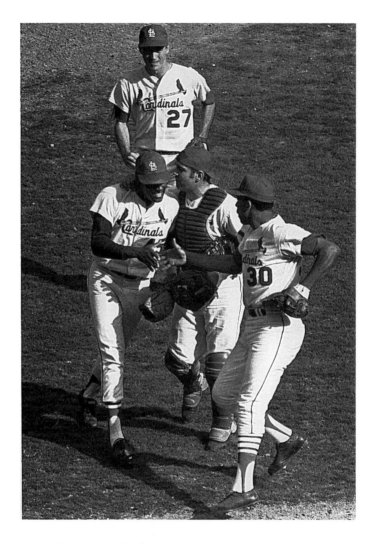

Catcher Tim McCarver and first baseman Orlando Cepeda congratulate Gibson after his record-setting, 17-strikeout performance in Game 1 of the 1968 World Series. Supremely focused on doing his job, Gibson merely shrugged when told about the record—he cared only about beating the Tigers, which he did by a score of 4–0.

merely scored four runs in each game he pitched, it might have been 30-2. "I've never seen a pitcher have a greater year," recalled Wes Parker. "He was on another planet."

Gibson kept it going into the World Series against the Tigers, starting with the 17-strike-out, 4–0 masterpiece in the opener. Gibson again defeated Denny McLain in Game 4, 10–1, giving St. Louis a three-games-to-one advantage. It was Gibson's seventh consecutive Series start with 10 or more strikeouts—a Fall Classic record. Gibson even hit his second World Series homer and was on his way to breaking his own record for strikeouts in one Series.

But like the Red Sox the year before, the Tigers rebounded to win the next two and send the Series to the seventh game. This time it would be Gibson versus Mickey Lolich, who had also won two games.

For six innings the two pitchers matched zeroes. Then, with two on and two out in the seventh, Gibson's year-long magic spell was snapped. Jim Northrup hit a fly ball toward center field that Curt Flood momentarily misjudged. ("If he can't catch it, nobody can," Gibson graciously said later.) The ball fell for a triple, and the Tigers had all the runs they would need. Symbolic of Gibson's hard-luck season, the Cards did not score until two were out in the ninth. They lost, 4–1.

Another autumn haul of honors for Gibson removed some of the sting from the World Series defeat. The *Sporting News* named him the league's Pitcher of the Year, also awarding him his fourth Gold Glove. On October 28, Gibson was unanimously selected as winner of the N.L. Cy Young Award, presented annually to the best pitcher in each league. And on November 13, he was named the National League's MVP, an honor rarely bestowed upon a pitcher.

At age 33, Bob Gibson had reached the top of his profession.

6

OPPONENTS ON AND OFF THE FIELD

Why don't you and the other blackbirds on the Cardinals move to Africa where you belong?" read the letter addressed to Bob Gibson. "If you and the other darkies can't read this because of your low mentality, get one of the white players to do it."

This is just a sampling of the mail received in 1968 by Gibson, a man deeply concerned with racial problems and not afraid to speak out against social injustice. The 1960s were a time of racial tension in the United States—perhaps more so than in any other era—climaxed by the 1968 assassination of civil rights leader Dr. Martin Luther King, Jr. Civil rights legislation came to long-overdue fruition in this decade, but a great many U.S. citizens were not ready or willing to accept the concept of racial equality.

Prejudice "happens every day of your life," said Gibson. "It's one of the underlying reasons why you are not accepted and respected the same as everyone else." His wife, Charline, acknowledged that the Gibsons had it better than many others, but she knew there was a

A dapper Gibson surveys the Manhattan street scene during a visit to New York in 1968. Gibson's dominant performance that year prompted changes in the rules to favor the hitters, but it did them little good against the Cardinals ace, who came back with yet another 20-win season in 1969.

specific reason. "If Bob and I are treated better than most blacks," said Charline, "it's only because he is a celebrity. It's a mark of our society that a man earns equality by throwing a baseball harder than someone else."

Gibson's ability to throw a baseball contributed to some changes in the game's rules for 1969. Pitchers had come to dominate the game for several seasons, and club owners and league officials worried that the lack of run production would cause fans to lose interest. The 1968 season was the clinching blow: major league batters hit just .236 as an aggregate, and teams averaged fewer than 3.5 runs per game. That winter, baseball's rules committee shrunk the strike zone by some 8 inches, and the pitcher's mound was lowered from an elevation of 15 inches to just 10. The effects were dramatic: within two years, big league scoring increased by 30 percent.

Even with the new rules, Gibson was hardly less effective in 1969. He completed 28 of 35 starts, working 314 innings. Although the Cardinals finished fourth out of the six teams in the newly formed N.L. Eastern Division, Gibson posted a 20-13 record with 269 strikeouts and a 2.18 ERA. And he accomplished all this despite an arthritic right elbow that had to be soaked in ice regularly. Gibson's arm was paying the price for years of rugged use and abuse. "I never pace myself," he once said. "I just go out there and give all I've got as long as I can."

The season produced many personal highlights. On March 3, Gibson signed a contract estimated at $125,000—five times the average major league salary that year—making him the highest-paid Cardinal of all time. On May 12, he tied a record by striking out three batters on a total of nine pitches in the seventh inning of a 6–2 win over the Dodgers. In June he made his 53rd consecutive regular-season start without being removed while his team was still in the field. On July 13, he became the 20th pitcher ever to record 2,000 career strikeouts, victimizing Pittsburgh's Roberto Clemente. Gibson also earned his sixth All-Star selection and his fifth Gold Glove, and he even stole five bases—more than the majority of everyday players in the league that year.

Without the endless banquet circuit that often follows a pennant-winning season, Gibson was able to enjoy a quiet off-season for a change. He devoted much of it to his hobbies, which included playing the guitar, doing carpentry projects, and assembling model cars.

The 1970 season started out slowly for Gibson. By May 22, his record was just 2-3, accompanied by a horrendous 5.34 ERA. The next day, he struck out 16 Phillies to start a 10-game winning streak, including a 7-0 record in June. On June 17, he shut out the San Diego Padres, 8–0, striking out 13 and coming within four outs of a no-hit game. It was one of 35 times in his career Gibson allowed three hits or fewer in a complete game, but he had never quite achieved that masterpiece every pitcher hopes for. "I don't think I'll ever pitch a no-hitter," he often said, "because I'm a high-ball pitcher."

Gibson made the N.L. All-Star Team in July and was named the league's Player of the Month in August after going 6-0 in the midst of a seven-game winning streak. On September 6 he earned his 20th victory, becoming the first Cardinal ever to notch five 20-win seasons.

By the end of the year, Gibson's won-lost mark was a splendid 23-7; in contrast, the

Charline Gibson applauds her husband during the 1967 World Series in Boston's Fenway Park. Despite their comfortable life-style, Charline and Bob Gibson were both deeply concerned about racial injustice in the United States, and they spoke out forcefully on the subject many times.

record of the rest of the Cardinals staff was 53-79, with no teammate winning more than 10 games. Gibson hurled 294 innings and completed 23 games, setting career highs in victories and strikeouts (274). He thus became the first man ever to amass eight 200-strikeout seasons.

Gibson also continued to excel in batting and fielding, winning another Gold Glove and collecting 33 hits, 19 RBIs, and a .303 average. But it was for his mound work that Gibson was named the winner of the N.L.'s Cy Young Award (receiving 23 of 24 first-place votes) and the *Sporting News*'s Pitcher of the Year citation. Other post-season honors included the Missouri Athletic Club's Sports Personality of the Year; the St. Louis Baseball Man of the Year Award; and the Atlanta Booster organization's Pitcher of the Year. Perhaps the biggest prize came at the end of the season, when Gibson signed a 1971 pact for $150,000—the richest player contract ever to that point.

Charline Gibson also earned some money from baseball. With Michael Rich, she coauthored *A Wife's Guide to Baseball* for Viking Press. The book described the fundamentals and subtleties of the game in a chatty style and contained some expert commentary from Charline's husband.

The 1971 season was not one of Gibson's best. He spent 21 days on the disabled list in late spring with a torn right thigh muscle, and by July 21, his record was a disappointing 6-9 with a 3.90 ERA. Despite rebounding to go 10-4 and 2.12 thereafter, he finished with his worst won-lost mark since 1962.

On the other hand, few seasons produced as many milestones for Gibson as this one. On August 4 he recorded his 200th career victory, a

7–2 win over the Giants. On September 12 he notched his 50th lifetime shutout, a four-hit, 4–0 whitewash of the Cubs. And in between, he finally got that elusive no-hit game.

As Gibson was on his way to Pittsburgh's Three Rivers Stadium on August 14, a young boy asked him, "Are you going to shut out Pittsburgh tonight?" Gibson, a proud but not boastful man, answered yes. Later, he predicted to teammate Joe Torre, "I think I'll throw a no-hitter tonight." By the end of the evening, Gibson had fulfilled his forecast: a no-hit game against a hard-hitting team on its way to the 1971 world championship. Gibson struck out 10 Pirates, and he even drove in three runs in the 11–0 masterpiece. Three weeks later, the Cards honored Gibson in pregame ceremonies, giving him a gold ring that featured his uniform number, 45, displayed in diamonds.

Although Gibson's 16-13 record was unimposing, he tied for the N.L. lead with five shutouts and had a lower ERA than in his Cy Young season of 1970. He won his seventh consecutive Gold Glove Award and helped the Cards to a second-place finish, their best in three years of divisional play.

Gibson's off-season activities included a 17-day tour of military hospitals in Guam, the Philippines, Japan, and Okinawa. He also got a taste of baseball broadcasting, covering the National League Championship Series between the Pirates and the Giants; it was not his first time behind the mike; he had broadcasted college basketball for WOW-TV in Nebraska and WPIX-TV in New York. To some observers, it might have suggested that he was already thinking about life after baseball.

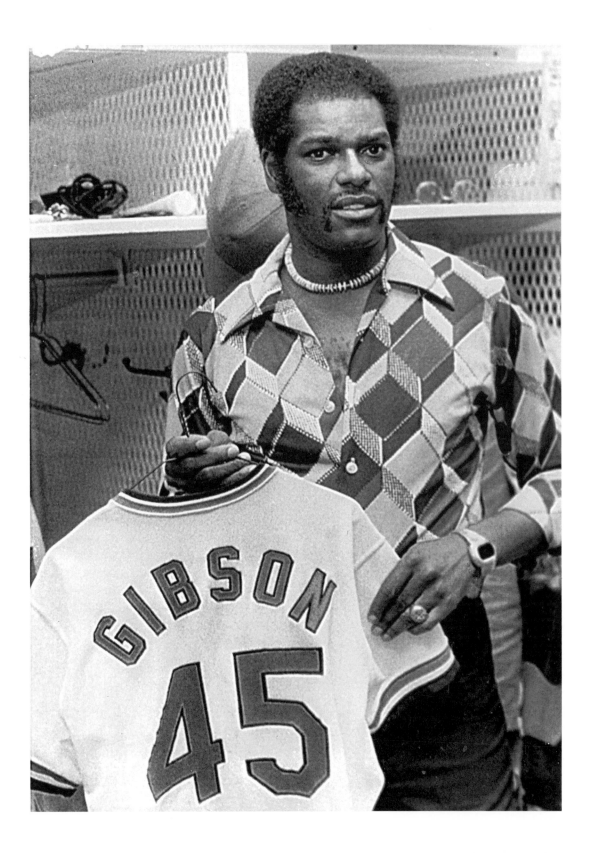

7

THE TWILIGHT YEARS

In a pattern that was becoming all too familiar, Bob Gibson started the 1972 season slowly. A players' strike had delayed the season by 13 days, and by May 24 Gibson still had not earned a victory. He had suffered five losses to go along with a 4.45 ERA.

Finally came the first win, a 4–2 triumph over Pittsburgh. Then another victory, a third, and a fourth. After two straight starts were rained out came the biggest win of all: Gibson's 14–3 triumph over the Padres on June 21 not only evened his record at 5-5 but also made him the winningest pitcher in St. Louis Cardinals history. (Hall of Famer Jesse Haines, who finished with 210 wins, had been the record holder since 1929.)

Gibson's win streak stretched to 11 games, during which time his ERA was a minuscule 1.39. He was picked to start the 1972 All-Star Game in Atlanta, the eighth time he had made the team but the first All-Star start of his illustrious career. In what was to be his final appearance in the Midsummer Classic, Gibson hurled

Gibson hangs up his uniform for the last time on September 18, 1975, following a subpar season. After amassing 251 wins and 3,117 strikeouts, the 39-year-old right-hander decided that it was time to move on.

Gibson writhes in pain during a 1973 game after trying to pitch with a torn knee cartilage. He returned from surgery to pitch effectively, but even he admitted that "physical and mental stresses" were beginning to take their toll.

two scoreless innings to start the National League off to a 4–3 win. In all, Gibson appeared in six All-Star contests, tossing 11 innings with 10 strikeouts and a 3.27 ERA, but no wins or losses.

Over the last 19 weeks of the regular season, Gibson was in his old form, going 19-6, with the strike having cost him a shot at another 20-win season. Gibson completed 23 games (in an average time of 1 hour, 56 minutes) and fanned 208 batters—his ninth 200-strikeout season (a record later broken by Tom Seaver and Nolan Ryan). But despite his efforts, the Cardinals dropped back to fourth place.

Gibson signed his 1973 contract for $160,000 but once again got off to a rocky start. His record was 3-6 as of June 5, but then things started turning around. First, he broke Red Ruffing's major league record of 242 consecutive starting assigments. (He would extend the record to 303 by 1975, but Steve Carlton would later surpass it.) On June 11, Gibson became the number two strikeout pitcher of all time, passing Jim Bunning with K number 2,856 during a 12–4 win over Cincinnati. On June 21, Gibson "called his shot" in the Babe Ruth tradition, homering against the Montreal Expos after predicting he would and helping himself to a 4–3 win; five weeks later, Gibson hit his final career homer, a grand slam against the Mets.

By August 4, Gibson had boosted his record

to 11-10, and the Cardinals had risen from a 5-20 start to first place in the N.L. East. Then disaster hit. While running the bases in a game against New York, Gibson suffered torn cartilage in his right knee. In character, he tried to resume pitching but collapsed on the mound. Surgery was performed, and many people wondered if Bob Gibson—nearing 38 years of age—would ever pitch again.

Gibson was out for eight weeks, during which time the Cards went 20-31. Then, on the next-to-last day of the season, Gibson made a dramatic comeback, pitching six innings of a 7–1 win over the Phillies. It was not enough: the Cards finished 1½ games behind the pennant-winning Mets.

Gibson won his ninth and final Gold Glove Award in 1973 and finished the season 12-10 with a 2.77 ERA, despite the knee injury, a strained Achilles tendon in his other leg, and his chronically arthritic pitching elbow.

But Gibson's biggest problems came off the field. His Omaha home was vandalized four times in 1973. Then Charline Gibson, saying the couple's relationship was "irretrievably broken," sued for divorce. On January 22, 1974, the Gibsons' 16-year marriage was dissolved, with Charline receiving custody of the couple's two teenage daughters, plus child support, alimony, and a division of the couple's property.

Having difficulty pushing off his damaged right knee—from which fluid was drained 22 times in 1974—Gibson struggled to a 3-8 record and a 5.17 ERA through June 23. He came back to go 8-5 the rest of the season but still finished with his first losing year since 1960. The Cardinals again missed the N.L. East title by just 1½ games.

The season did contain one highlight, however. On July 17, Gibson struck out Cincinnati's Cesar Geronimo to become the second pitcher in big league history to amass 3,000 career strikeouts. A St. Louis crowd of 28,473 gave him a standing ovation, and he later received the J. Roy Stockton Award for his achievement.

Gibson signed his final player contract on January 27, 1975, accepting a pay cut. "My years with the Cardinals have been as happy and enjoyable as any individual could expect," he said, "and I feel that I've made and will make one more contribution to Cardinal teams . . . but it's getting time to quit. An athlete reaches a point where the physical and mental stresses begin to work against him."

After compiling a good 2.81 ERA in spring training, Gibson struck out 12 Expos on opening day—but lost. By the end of May, he was 1-5 with a bloated ERA, a start reminiscent of those of the previous five seasons. But this time there was no remarkable turnaround. This time, Gibson was an injury-plagued 39-year-old pitcher. And this time, he was removed from the Cardinals' starting rotation. "I think they're making a mistake," Gibson said of the demotion, but the writing was on the wall.

Gibson pitched only 43 more innings the rest of the year, occasionally starting, more often relieving, and showing only brief flashes of his former excellence. Against Montreal on June 27, he recorded his 250th career victory. One month later, he hurled four scoreless relief innings against Philadelphia to earn his last big league win. He had two saves in August, made his final appearance on September 3, and left the team for good 15 days later.

On September 1, 1975, a sellout crowd of

Gibson (center) listens as St. Louis general manager Red Schoendienst addresses the Cardinals squad during spring training in 1975. The star pitcher had signed a $150,000 contract that winter, making him the highest-paid player in baseball.

48,435 came to Busch Memorial Stadium for Bob Gibson Day. Gibson's uniform was retired, and his locker was presented to the St. Louis Sports Hall of Fame. A bust of Gibson was unveiled, a telegram from President Gerald Ford was read, and a motor home was presented to the pitcher as a gift. "It's both a sad day and a proud day," said Cardinals owner August A. Busch. "It's sad because it marks the end of one of the greatest baseball careers of all time. But it's a proud day to say, 'Bob Gibson, you have done a great job. You're a symbol of what it means to work hard.' "

"One thing that I've always been proud of," Gibson said in his own speech, "is the fact that I've never intentionally cheated anybody out of what they paid their money to come and see. But most of all I'm proud of the fact that whatever I did, I did it my way."

Bob Gibson completed his career with a record of 251–174, with 3,117 strikeouts, 56 shutouts, and a 2.91 ERA. In World Series competition he was 7–2 with a 1.89 ERA.

"In my 21 seasons I never saw a better pitcher or competitor," said all-time home run and RBI king Henry Aaron. "If I had a game to win, I'd take Gibby."

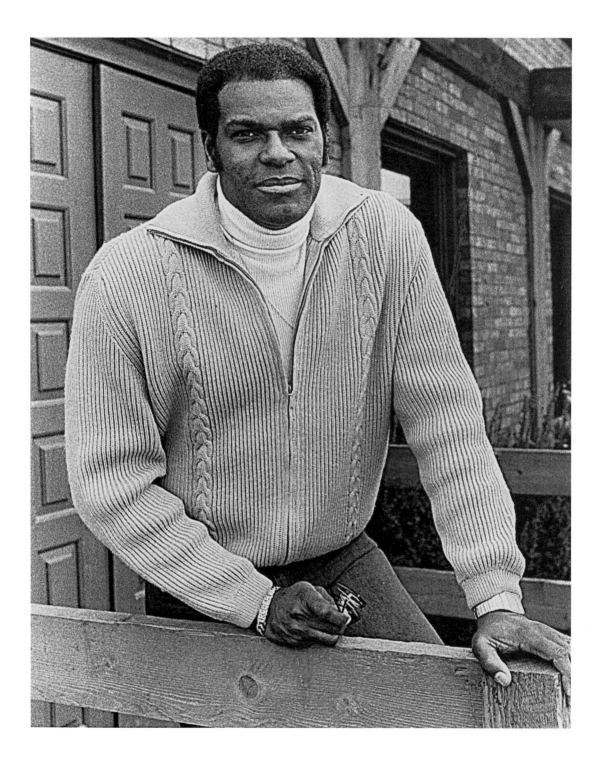

8
NEW VENTURES

One of Bob Gibson's first ventures as a retired player was to become a baseball announcer. In 1976, he joined Al Michaels and Norm Cash in the broadcast booth, doing play-by-play for ABC-TV. All seemed to be going well until Gibson was unexpectedly thrust into his first on-field interview on August 9. Pittsburgh's John Candelaria had just pitched a no-hit game, and Gibson was sent down to capture the moment for the millions of television viewers.

The interview was a disaster. Gibson asked inappropriate questions, missed cues, and went out of his way to remind everyone that he himself had once pitched a no-hitter. The print media blasted Gibson for his "incompetence," and his short-lived ABC career was soon over.

But Gibson had several other irons in the fire. In April 1973, he and several associates had opened the Community Bank of Nebraska in Omaha, for which Gibson served as chairman of the board. In 1976, Gibson opened a restaurant and bar—called Bob Gibson's for Spirits and Sustenance—in his hometown. Gibson was also a majority stockholder in KOWH, an Omaha soul-music radio station and was involved with firms that invested in real estate.

Adjusting to life without baseball, Gibson tries to look casual in front of his spacious Omaha home—but the competitive fire still burns in his eyes. Seeking new challenges, the retired hurler became a baseball announcer for ABC and invested in several businesses in his hometown.

Missing the excitement and camaraderie of baseball, Gibson signed on as a pitching coach with the New York Mets in 1981. In this spring-training session, he shows Tim Leary how to vary his grip on the ball: the New York pitchers showed improvement under his tutelage, but unfortunately for the Mets, none of them became another Bob Gibson.

Gibson soon realized that he was not cut out for desk jobs. He missed the camaraderie, action, and drama of baseball. When former teammate Joe Torre offered him a coaching job with the New York Mets, Gibson jumped at the chance. Torre was manager of the Mets at the time, and Gibson joined him as the team's assistant pitching and "attitude" coach for the 1981 season.

The Mets staff ERA dropped from 3.85 to 3.55 in 1981, but the team still managed to finish in its usual spot near the basement. Torre was fired, and Gibson went with him. When Torre was signed to manage the Atlanta Braves for the following season, he wasted no time in asking Gibson to join him again.

The Braves had not finished higher than fourth place in the N.L. West since 1974, but under Torre and his coaching staff the club surprised everyone by winning the divisional title in 1982. Following second-place finishes in both 1983 and 1984, however, Braves owner Ted Turner fired Torre and his crew. The team subsequently dropped to fifth place in 1985 and did not rise to the top again until 1991.

With his four-year coaching career over, Gibson went on to other things. He resumed broadcasting in 1985, with KMOX radio in St. Louis. The following year, he joined the old-timers series sponsored by Equitable Insurance. The series features retired baseball stars playing entertaining, low-competition exhibition games around the country, and it is designed to raise money for financially troubled former players.

The highlight of Gibson's retirement came in 1981. On January 14, it was announced that he had been elected to the National Baseball Hall of Fame in Cooperstown, New York, in his very first try. Needing 75 percent of the votes, Gibson was named on 337 of 401 ballots, a resounding 84 percent. This was remarkable for three reasons. First, the competition was fierce: the ballot included future Hall of Famers Don Drysdale, Harmon Killebrew, Hoyt Wilhelm, Juan Marichal, Red Schoendienst, and Luis Aparicio, none of whom made it in 1981. Second, only 15

After being inducted into the Baseball Hall of Fame on August 2, 1981, Gibson shares his feelings with the fans and the media. Beyond his dazzling career statistics, Bob Gibson is remembered as a supreme clutch performer. "If I had a game to win," home run king Henry Aaron once said, "I'd take Gibby."

players—and just five pitchers—had previously been elected on their first try. Finally, the people doing the voting were baseball writers, with whom Gibson had long had strained relations. Nevertheless, the vast majority of these writers realized that whether they loved or hated him, Bob Gibson belonged in the Hall of Fame with the other greats of baseball history.

Tributes came from all over. On February 2, Gibson's election was officially recognized in the Proceedings of the 97th Congress. Shortly after,

Gibson was honored at Bob Gibson Hall of Fame Day in Omaha.

On August 2, 1981, Gibson was formally inducted into the Hall, along with Johnny Mize, an old-time slugger, and the late Rube Foster, a Negro Leagues pioneer. Gibson, out of character, broke down during his acceptance speech.

"Playing baseball was my life, and it's something I devoted 100 percent to," said Gibson. "I want to be remembered as a person, a competitor, that gave 100 percent every time I went out on the field."

As Gibson entered his mid-fifties, he was living in the Omaha suburb of Bellevue, Nebraska, with his second wife, Wendy. During the baseball season, he broadcast games for ESPN, the national cable TV network. The rest of the time he was inclined to guard his privacy, rarely answering fan mail and avoiding public functions. In that respect Gibson had not changed much over the years. "I owe the fans 100 percent on the field, and I give them exactly that," he said during his playing days. "Anything else I give is completely up to me." No one who saw him pitch would be inclined to argue with Bob Gibson.

CHRONOLOGY

1935	Born Robert Gibson in Omaha, Nebraska, on November 9
1954	Enters Creighton University on a basketball scholarship
1957	Marries Charline Marie Johnson; signs contract to play professional baseball with the Omaha Cardinals in the American Association
1959	Makes major league debut for the St. Louis Cardinals on April 15, pitching in relief against the Los Angeles Dodgers; earns first major league victory on July 30, 1–0 over the Cincinnati Reds
1961	Leads National League right-handed pitchers in ERA with 3.24
1962	Ties for N.L. lead with five shutouts and is selected to All-Star Team for the first time
1964	Leads Cardinals to their first pennant in 18 years; wins two games in World Series against the Yankees, including the clincher, and is named Series MVP
1965	Enjoys first 20-win season
1967	Wins three World Series games against the Red Sox, earning his second Series MVP Award
1968	Enjoys his finest season, winning 22 games (including 15 in a row) with a 1.12 ERA, the lowest in 50 years; wins N.L. Cy Young Award and MVP Award
1970	Achieves career-high victory total (23); becomes first pitcher to record 200 or more strikeouts for eight seasons; wins second Cy Young Award
1971	Pitches no-hitter against Pittsburgh Pirates on August 14; notches 50th career shutout against Chicago Cubs on September 12; wins seventh consecutive Gold Glove Award
1972	Records 211th career victory on June 21, becoming all-time Cardinals leader in wins
1974	Chalks up 3,000th career strikeout on July 17
1975	Defeats Montreal Expos on June 27 for 250th career victory; announces his retirement and is honored at Bob Gibson Day in St. Louis on September 1
1981	Inducted into the Baseball Hall of Fame

ROBERT GIBSON
ST. LOUIS N.L., 1959-1975.

FIVE-TIME 20-GAME WINNER. HIS 3,117
STRIKEOUTS MADE HIM ONLY 2ND PITCHER TO
REACH 3,000. FIRST TO FAN 200 OR MORE IN
A SEASON 9 TIMES. SET N.L. MARK WITH 1.12
ERA IN 1968, HURLING 13 SHUTOUTS. TWICE
WORLD SERIES MVP, SETTING RECORDS FOR
CONSECUTIVE VICTORIES (7), CONSECUTIVE
COMPLETE GAMES (8), AND STRIKEOUTS IN A
GAME (17) AND A SERIES (35). VOTED N.L.
MVP IN 1968 AND CY YOUNG AWARD WINNER IN
1968 AND 1970. WON NINE GOLD GLOVE AWARDS.

MAJOR LEAGUE STATISTICS

ST. LOUIS CARDINALS

YEAR	TEAM	W	L	PCT	ERA	G	GS	CG	IP	H	BB	SO	ShO
1959	ST.L N	3	5	.375	3.33	13	9	2	75.2	77	39	48	1
1960		3	6	.333	5.61	27	12	2	86.2	97	48	69	0
1961		13	12	.520	3.24	35	27	10	211.1	186	119	166	2
1962		15	13	.536	2.85	32	30	15	233.2	174	95	208	5
1963		18	9	.667	3.39	36	33	14	254.2	224	96	204	2
1964		19	12	.613	3.01	40	36	17	287.1	250	86	245	2
1965		20	12	.625	3.07	38	36	20	299.0	243	103	270	6
1966		21	12	.636	2.44	35	35	20	280.1	210	78	225	5
1967		13	7	.650	2.98	24	24	10	175.1	151	40	147	2
1968		22	9	.710	1.12	34	34	28	304.2	198	62	268	13
1969		20	13	.606	2.18	35	35	28	314.0	251	95	269	4
1970		23	7	.767	3.12	34	34	23	294.0	262	88	274	3
1971		16	13	.552	3.04	31	31	20	245.2	215	76	185	5
1972		19	11	.633	2.46	34	34	23	278.0	226	88	208	4
1973		12	10	.545	2.77	25	25	13	195.0	159	57	142	1
1974		11	13	.458	3.83	33	33	9	240.0	236	104	129	1
1975		3	10	.231	5.04	22	14	1	109.0	120	62	60	0
Totals		251	174	.591	2.91	528	482	255	3884.1	3279	1336	3117	56

World Series

YEAR	TEAM	W	L	PCT	ERA	G	GS	CG	IP	H	BB	SO	ShO
1964		2	1	.666	3.00	3	3	2	27	23	8	31	0
1967		3	0	1.000	1.00	3	3	3	27	14	5	26	0
1968		2	1	.666	1.67	3	3	3	27	18	4	35	1
Totals		7	2	.777	1.89	9	9	8	81	55	17	92	1

FURTHER READING

Berkow, Ira. "Gibson: Do Fans Ask Too Much of Athletes?" *Washington Daily News*, July 22, 1969.

Broeg, Bob. "Bob Gibson: Baseball's Toughest Pitcher." *Baseball Digest*, April 1971.

Gibson, Bob, with Phil Pepe. *From Ghetto to Glory: The Story of Bob Gibson*. Englewood Cliffs, NJ: Prentice Hall, 1968.

Hano, Arnold. "Bob Gibson: Symbol of a New Breed." *Sport*, May 1968.

Herman, Jack. "Bob Gibson, Flame-Thrower, Adds Fire Control." *Baseball Digest*, September 1962.

Hirt, Clyde. "Is Gibson Number One Pitcher?" *All Sports*, September 1971.

Hummel, Rick. "Mellow Bob Gibson." *Sporting News*, August 8, 1981.

Katz, Fred. "Bob Gibson: A Man Who Challenges You in Every Way." *Sport*, July 1971.

Lipman, David, and Ed Wilks. *Bob Gibson: Pitching Ace*. New York: Putnam, 1975.

Russo, Neal. "Doubters Climb on Gibson Bandwagon." *Sporting News*, October 31, 1964.

Terry, Dickson. "Gibson a Riddle on and off the Field." *Sporting News*, October 28, 1967.

Vecsey, George. "How Far Can Gibson Go?" *Sport*, July 1965.

Wilks, Ed. "Bob Gibson's Secret Battle Against Disaster." *Super Sports*, March 1969.

INDEX

PICTURE CREDITS
National Baseball Library, Cooperstown, NY: pp. 56, 60; *Sporting News*: p. 58; Sports Photo Source: pp. 12, 15; UPI/Bettmann: pp. 2, 8, 11, 18, 21, 24, 26, 28, 30, 31, 32, 36, 38, 40, 44, 46, 48, 51, 52, 54.

BILL DEANE is the author of *Award Voting*, for which he won the 1989 SABR-Macmillan Baseball Research Award. He has also contributed to numerous baseball periodicals and reference books. Born in Poughkeepsie, New York, he moved upstate to become senior research associate for the National Baseball Hall of Fame in Cooperstown. Bill Deane lives in Fly Creek, New York, with his wife, Pam, and his daughter, Sarah.

JIM MURRAY, veteran sports columnist of the *Los Angeles Times*, is one of America's most acclaimed writers. He has been named "America's Best Sportswriter" by the National Association of Sportscasters and Sportswriters 14 times, was awarded the Red Smith Award, and was twice winner of the National Headliner Award. In addition, he was awarded the J. G. Taylor Spink Award in 1987 for "meritorious contributions to baseball writing." With this award came his 1988 induction into the National Baseball Hall of Fame in Cooperstown, New York. In 1990, Jim Murray was awarded the Pulitzer Prize for Commentary.

EARL WEAVER is the winningest manager in the Baltimore Orioles history by a wide margin. He compiled 1,480 victories in his 17 years at the helm. After managing eight different minor league teams, he was given the chance to lead the Orioles in 1968. Under his leadership the Orioles finished lower than second place in the American League East only four times in 17 years. One of only 12 managers in big league history to have managed in four or more World Series, Earl was named Manager of the Year in 1979. The popular Weaver had his number 5 retired in 1982, joining Brooks Robinson, Frank Robinson, and Jim Palmer, whose numbers were retired previously. Earl Weaver continues his association with the professional baseball scene by writing, broadcasting, and coaching.